# Small Small Joys

# Small Small Joys

Shubh Schiesser

*atmosphere press*

Published by Atmosphere Press

Cover design by Ronaldo Alves



Atmospherepress.com

To my beloved children,
Era and Amitabh

# Contents

## 1


Bathing Spree 5
Is it You? 6
Royal Iris 8
Aladdin's Lamp 9
Undertow 10
Fabric of Disquiet 11
Leaves 12
Pear Blossoms in Spring 13
Spellbound 14
My Friday Night Lights 15
Soaring 16
Night Thieves 17
The Doe's Message 19
Leaf Peeping in Stowe, Vermont 20
Hill Country Sonata 21
Greetings From Wimberley 22
New Beginning 23


## 2


The Spa Ritual 27
Sakura 28
Tokyo Earthquake 29

The Fisherman 31
Mother's Love 33
Turquoise 34
Mango Delight 35
Magic Shoes 36
Sandalwood Solstice 39
Small Small Joys 41
Charm of an Indian Monsoon 42
Malarial Vampire 43
Rose Bud Dream 44
Grandmother's Song 45
Sari 46
Forced Marriage 47
Indian Widow 49
Ebullience 51
No 52
Before It Breaks 53
A Broken Kite 54
Beyond Closed Doors 56
Pain 57
Sweet Feeling of Freedom 58

**3**

Prom 63
Chasm 64
Restless Descents 65
Crab Constellation 66
Season of Thorns 67

Melancholy 68
Frame of Mind 69
Microburst 70
At Last 71
Vertigo 72
Purple Asters 73
Above McKinney Falls, Austin, TX 74
The Smile 75
I Own Her 76
My Best Friends During the Pandemic 79
Garden Within a Garden, Zilker Park 81
Untitled Poem 82

**Epilogue**

Ode to My Teacher 85

Notes 87

# Foreword

***A note from the author***

Nature is all around us, subtle, quiet, loud and forceful. I find it deeply healing. My poetry collection is a bouquet of delicate flowers, but not without thorns. Some of my poems are pointed—portraying the angst of Indian women, coming from a patriarchal society—which I don't want to ignore. Hope you find meaning in my words—simple, but from the heart.

# 1

# Bathing Spree

A drift of swans
twitter and chatter
across the ruffled
surface of a pond

Some cygnets
dive up and down
playing a game
peek-a-boo

Others toss their heads
nonchalantly
flapping their feathers
and preening

Then, in unison
they all clamber ashore
and, ladylike, walk away
swinging their hips provocatively

# Is it You?

At night
before I slept
cicada songs reinforced my
dreams of meeting you

Embracing you I gasped
Finally I had you in my arms
God            what blessings
How my heart labored…

I knew then what happiness was
just as an artist
knows love by painting on silk…
layers and layers of red

Moments stretched out
Nothing mattered except
oneness
palpable warmth

Quickly came the time for good-byes
Romance faded like
star moths beating the windows while
tears trembled

until my heart
vibrated
wildly like
xylophone bars

Your face danced in my eyes
Zen-like my mind stood still.

# Royal Iris

Your golden-spotted eye
responds to the salute of crew-cut grass

Bougainvillea and crepe myrtles
bend a curtsy to your splendor

Breezes caress your cheeks
Green slender leaves ripple like ribbons

Yellow lantana clings to your feet
holding you steady to the loamy soil

The melody of starstruck bees
The taste of dew on your periphery

No weed dares raise its head in your presence
Only a ladybug aches to clamber your stem

# Aladdin's Lamp

In my fist a flash of fireflies
I release them one by one
but hold one afloat
I have Aladdin's lamp

I release them one by one
watch them glow against nature's dark crepe
flitting in and out of rosemary bushes

but hold one afloat
it blinks like a golden star
winks at the moon

I have Aladdin's lamp
a borrowed beam of light
O enchanter my heart brightens

# Undertow

The careless wind
drives waves onto the shore
and churns them white
Who thinks the foam is snow?

drives waves onto the shore
where the bellows blow
the sand into the sea

and churns them white
breaks apart the reflection
of lapis sky

Who thinks the foam is snow?
when froth
hides the turmoil below

# Fabric of Disquiet

Sundown smears
golden patches
on treetops

Evening's breath
whirls through foliage
Wind chimes clatter

Fallen leaves
rise up like ballerinas
in swift pirouette

Night drops
into an enormous net
seizes thoughts in its web

Memories open
an attic in the dark canopy
torn by shooting stars

# Leaves

In autumn
you wear brown
drop
from woody branches

In damp soil
you sleep in the lap of roots
the warmth
of their black cocoon

In spring
you wake to stretch
tender shoots
delicate veins under the moon

then you
seesaw with dew
lick moonshine
while it floats on your lips

# Pear Blossoms in Spring

Ecstatic
as dragonfly's wings
sprayed by a wispy breeze
on the grassy yard
a welcoming pathway
for a wandering bride

The moon glides
in her satiny gown
beams
on the glossy branches

then rises into clouds
above
a serenade of crickets
and night birds

# Spellbound

Blue tiles cobble
the slippery path
to the park in Sintra Valley

Bougainvillea blazes red
against azaleas' fuchsia
and lilies' lavender
while an emerald parakeet circles
in the musky olives

I stand beneath the canopy
mystified and stretch both arms,
twirl like a dervish in an ecstatic state

Sintra Valley, Lisbon, Portugal

# My Friday Night Lights

Lost in the mysteries of dusk
a caravan of fireflies
emerges from the jasmine bush
and covers my courtyard fence

Then like a court jester, the first
announces a brief show
Soon hundreds more shimmer in the dark
Swirling, whirling, flashing
splashes of gold
beneath the sky's diamonds

They disappear in thick bushes
Reappear in a bonfire of light
throbbing like my heart

# Soaring

My heart is a bird
seeking heights
dreaming
soaring into an open sky

Seeking heights
far above the green trees
in a jungle of clouds

Dreaming
racing with twists of breeze
where ocean is stitched to the sky

Soaring into an open sky
where my wings expand
until my spirit settles on a sickle moon

# Night Thieves

They come
armed on starry nights
with bulldozers
slicing though the greenery
on both sides of Manchaca Road

They fail
to see the flush of birds roused
from their deep sleep
or hear the whine of nervous insects
the grumble of critters in tree bark

They shave
the bristle off the land,
leave behind soft ochre
sand smooth
as a baseball diamond

They erect matchbox pads
like pigeon holes
one on top of another
Then a banner appears:

one bedroom
        two bedrooms
                free cable
one month utilities included

# The Doe's Message

Her smooth bronze coat
is tightly stitched to a graceful body,
lanky and muscular legs
light and swift like a ballet dancer
Her tail is a bell flower in the wind

Her face points towards me
Large almond-shaped eyes
wide-set on her conic face—
the eyes of Nefertiti, outlined with khol
innocent and seductive

Our eyes meet
*This is our domain*
*Where our clan and babies roam*
Do I hear her?

She raises her wide eyes
turns her back
and turns again to see me
then gambols fast
disappearing in the thicket

# Leaf Peeping in Stowe, Vermont

Rounded green hills
metamorph
into vermillion and vibrant amber

Tall maples
drenched in honey
orange and deep red

Mighty oaks and ginkgoes
embrace each other tightly
Trapped air turns into amber wine

From the gondola on Mansfield Mountain
cirrus clouds at arm's length
Down below, a calm enchantment of rusty forest

On the slopes of the green valley
a gregarious flock of sheep gossips
while baby lambs and a yearling jump and jump

in the fold. As the veil of fog
wraps the trees and their magical carpet,
I warm myself beside a hearth

# Hill Country Sonata

Bald cypress trees
fret both sides of the creek
their bare branches spread
like a black filigree shawl
covering sunset

The stream hums
festive carols played
on keys of roots
entertains the lonely
hermits of winter

# Greetings From Wimberley

A chalice moon overflows
spilling light onto three iron
frogs standing in the doorway
of Creek Haven Inn
One has a flute
the second a guitar
and the third drums
Their fedoras vibrate with each burst
of *happy new year*
piped through their open mouths

Under the starburst sky
a ceramic fish spouts water
into a pond creating ripples
teased into wide circles
by the zephyr wind

Bronze and copper leaves dance
across the expanse of lawn
They too murmur
*happy new year*
before resting for auld lang syne

# New Beginning

A shiny film
paints the leaves
where spiders wrote

The sun's eye
beckons me
outside

A diamond
in a cherry tree
just for me

# 2

# The Spa Ritual

Tall bamboo peeked at my nakedness
through the veil of willows
surrounding the hot pool

My clothes melted
under the shine of a harvest moon
puddle at my feet
as I stepped towards my frolicking friends

*Au naturel* is not easy I learned
If I covered my breasts with a washcloth
down there would be uncovered
And if I covered down there
my upper part…

Despite the leering moon
the chorus of cicadas
lulled me into a trance

Oyama-san said:
let's rub each other's backs
with washcloths
to strengthen our friendship
an old Japanese custom

It was easy from then on

Tokyo, Japan

# Sakura

A twinkle of pinky white buds
announce spring in Tokyo
Cluster of creamy petals
hide shy tender greens

The fluid skins of petals flicker
in wavering sunlight
Sky stoops to press branches
to the emperor's moat

Blue jays intoxicated by spring's suddenness
dangle like jewels from the branches
The old and feeble are wheeled
from homes to enjoy Sakura

Bouquets of people under trees
drink sake and play flute songs
Giggling girls in kimonos sing *Sakura*
Their voices echo in Shinto shrine bells

Tokyo, Japan

# Tokyo Earthquake

A loud rumble from earth's belly
pushes waves violently
The bathing tub rocks

a boat in high waves
My traumatized, post-operative body
is fearful. I try to get up

but am pushed back into the tub,
caught in the turmoil
I hold the tub's edges

and tumble onto the trembling floor
too weak to pull the towels
I crawl for a pillow to cover my head

slip under the dresser panicked
Outside the windows electric
and telephone wires spasm

elliptically
Sounds of falling paintings
dishes cracking on the floor

Then I hear
*Reach - Safe - Hurry - to the Peace Park*
one mile away from my house

I am naked and cannot run
My heartbeat like a time bomb

Tokyo, Japan

# The Fisherman

Era and Amit skittered merrily
like shore birds in the cool sand
at the skirt of a retreating tide

The retreating tide that beckoned
with its foamy lips
*come and play with me*

*swim swim*
*into my waiting arms*

*Come back Era*, Amit shouted
into the pounding surf
don't go so far, so very far
away from mama and me

Era's outstretched arms were mere sticks
bobbing and bobbing in the waves,
her voice lost in the sky

*mama come.... help....*
Like a panicked gull I plunged
into the surf but stopped short when I heard

Amit begging me from the shore
*don't leave me mama, come back to me*

The shroud of night covered Era
as the currents pulled her
out of sight like a fish
in Neptune's net

*Is it God's plan?* I cried
*should Era be taken away from us?*

Then a young man appeared
and touched my shoulder before
struggling into the waves
that seemed too strong, too strong

for a mortal man to fight
I watched him through my tears
until he finally brought Era to my lap

I melted her with my kisses
When I looked up to thank her savior
he had already disappeared into an advancing
fog

Abu Dhabi, Capital of the United Arab Emirates

# Mother's Love

He was an axis of his mother's life
fell in love with an exciting girl
who demanded proof of love--his mother's heart
He must pluck the heart from beneath maternal
breasts

He fell in love with an exciting girl
she was jealous of his mother
intolerant of his divided attention

To prove his love she demanded his mother's
heart
such a price to prove his devotion
but he was eager to please his love

He plucked the heart from beneath his mother's
breasts
He pulled it free but stumbled when the heart
tumbled
in the dust, when it cried *are you hurting, my son?*

# Turquoise

Turquoise arose from indigo
indigo from violet
violet from teal
a blend of blue - green
aqua azure and aquamarine

Turquoise lines the water and sky
where Krishna dances
around azure Yamuna River
a peacock feather tied on his blue forehead

When he breathes into his flute
beads of turquoise and lapis
enchant the *Gopis*
like I was charmed
by the turquoise pin
in my mother's nose

# Mango Delight

We sat in a circle on a genie's rug
with a bucketful of cold mangos
dipped in crushed iced water
*alfanso, langar, banarasi, dusehri, chausa*

Golden juice smooth fleshy
dripping nectar
tongues licking drops on fingers
seeds sucked and picked

When stomachs were filled
but greed still lingered
mother ordered
*enough iron for today*

She in a mango-colored sari
yellow   orange   red
embossed with mango motifs
sat in the open courtyard
busy with mango pickles
juicy spicy curries

tying fresh tender mango leaves
on the house doors
as good omens for the entire year

Delhi, India

# Magic Shoes

*"If you wear your right shoe on your left foot*
*and left shoe on your right*
*you will understand the mystery of magic"*
*—my father's words*

A magician appeared on the stage
in an Arabian maroon robe
his tapered mustaches tucked behind his ears
When he bowed his turban fell
and a ruby-eyed pigeon fluttered up
then a second, third, and fourth
circling over his head like a silver halo
*I looked at my shoes and closed my moist hands*

A young girl with blazing breasts appeared
with an open coffin    she hopped in
her master quickly bolted the lid
pulled a shining dagger from his waistband
and savagely plunged it after her
*I trembled and looked down at my switched*
*shoes*

Then his devilish hands cut the coffin in two
her head and legs separated

she was ruthlessly slaughtered
shocked silence
until the halves were joined
the lid opened
and the girl flew up like a butterfly
*my shoes    my shoes were failing me*
   *defeating me*

Like a leopard the magician leapt at the girl
forced her flat on a table
and waved his hands above her like a puppeteer
she rose from the table
until she was suspended in midair
like a paper boat
stationary, stiff, motionless
The magician looked out as if taunting me
with an absurd smirk he twirled his mustache
*my lips quivered*
*you beast    bring the girl down*
and I cursed my shoes

His hands moved like hysterical moths
as she returned to the table
where she sat like a bewildered child

screams of frenzy echoed in the hall
*o god what is wrong with my shoes*
*did I follow the instructions correctly?*

Later,  noticing my sullen face
father laughed loudly    kissed my head
opened his fist and a fire spark flashed
*Jugnu!* I shouted wide-eyed
*"Princess, this is magic too*
*you will understand later"*

Delhi, India

# Sandalwood Solstice

Vigorous oaks
shelter children
under leafy branches
their bicycles lie
horizontal in the grass
boys lift their t-shirts
a respite for
sweat-ridden bodies

In the yard
temperamental bees
burrow deep
in the center
of cornflowers
siphoning nectar
until blossoms
drop their petals

My unblemished heart
restless with summer heat
sandalwood aroma wafts
through the kitchen window

Summer moon in the sky
lurks behind the pear tree leaves
Its temporary spell
enchants me

# Small Small Joys

In Delhi's July heat
two sparrows drop in our courtyard
I sprinkle drops in their opened beaks

We sit on a straw mat under a noisy fan
Father rolls a big watermelon round and round
cooled under a midnight moon

A big bite makes rivers on both sides of my mouth
They flow down my arms trailing to the floor
I extend my left arm to greedy Romi for licking

Mother yells at us for spitting seeds on each other
Saliva-thick pips stick everyone's hair and faces
in the midst of house flies' annoying buzz

While our seed spitting competition is in full swing
Grandma orders me to collect all the rinds in a basket
to put outside the back door for wandering cows

Delhi, India

# Charm of an Indian Monsoon

Before the sky becomes an ebony blanket
and knots of lightning break through the clouds
ghosts of heat swarm

Sunrays are like prickly cactus
Birds drop dead with open mouths
and humans crumple like autumn leaves

The first rain is gentle, a mango shower—
delicate flowers are born on trees
rain coaxes buds into golden fruit

The second is heavy as syrup
the sweetness of relief
after the fatal heat

Soon, nature is a riot of green
the swollen Ganges glitters
Songs and anklets echo on swings

It is the time of fertility rites
Wives long for husbands who are far away
Fans inside rooms chirr like cicadas

Delhi, India

# Malarial Vampire

You thin-winged translucent phantom
You carry devilry in your tail

Your annoying buzz in my ears
swoops low as you pinch my arm
suck a bellyful of my fresh red blood

Your staggering belly enrages me
I smash you against the wall
leave a dirty stain on it

But you already have your revenge
My head pounds as I shiver with fever

Delhi, India

# Rose Bud Dream

A shy bud
observes a newly opened rose
dew trembles on fresh petals
Butterflies hover in perfumed air
Passersby stop to appreciate
the queen of flowers

The bud dreams
the day she will bloom too
rousing other flowers from sleep
at the sight of its scarlet blush
Honeybee wings will quiver
an intoxicating breeze will
carry golden pollen

A gardener interrupts
with a pair of scissors
Something rouses her
The garden will remain
but she will be alone
in a vase

Delhi, India

# Grandmother's Song

A paste of *haldi* and milk
is rubbed gently on my face
which takes a golden hue

I'm preparing for my wedding   my nuptials

I bathe my long hair in rose oil
red aboli and jasmine line my long plait
my hair is shining

I'm preparing for my wedding   my nuptials

Henna paste draws peacocks
on my hands   my hands and feet
decorated with jewels and in red silk

I'm ready for my wedding   my nuptials

Delhi, India

# Sari

Six yards of silk
sunset red, tangerine, papaya
whisper around her slender midriff
the true grace of her
heritage

When a breeze tugs
on her lime green sari
fields come alive
peacocks, parrots, marigolds, mangos
and
her loose *pallu* sails behind

Delhi, India

# Forced Marriage

Soon she will be the property
of a stranger—a master
who bought her like a sheep, goat or cow
from a village stockyard
with a nose ring and brass
bells ringing on her neck

Garlands of roses and jasmine
will soon turn pallid and stale.
The nose ring, forehead *tika* jewels
and fine silks will be memories of youth.
Sacred henna on her hands and feet
will wash away in no time

She will learn words and habits
of his harem: how to chisel her face,
how to wear a necklace of name-calling
when she forgets a button on his shirt,
hot water for his bath. When food
is not cooked to his taste, she will hear
dishes break while cracking the knuckles
of her clammy hands

Headaches and body-aches
will be taken as an excuse to shirk work.
She will stuff her *sari* in her mouth
to suppress cries.
She will age before getting old,
die before death

Delhi, India

# Indian Widow

Married women wrap her in a white sari
cover her freshly shaved head soon after
her husband's death, break her glass bangles
and wipe the red powder from her forehead
and the part of her hair

She must erase the memory of being married.
Now labeled an ill omen, an outcast,
a burden, jinxed, a taboo and a living
curse. Relatives shirk her
inauspicious face forever

She should be mindless, tongueless,
desireless, mirthless, spend her
remaining years in *Asrams* on the *ghats*
of Banaras near water and temples
with other unfortunates ones

She will eat once a day bland *satvic* food
to suppress and tame her appetite,
will bathe repeatedly to remain pure enough
to worship gods several times a day, begging
to forgive her harrowing journey of *karma*

Secretly, does she dream about her childhood?
Going to the carnival in princess finery
and being treated with sweets?

Benares, India

# Ebullience

The long night reigns without
a hint of surrender

Clouds float in patches
break the magic spells of stars

Dense sky is a tattered sheet
Stars in solitary aloofness

peep through holes
Moon reflects in muddy puddles

Some tears tremble like slender reeds
at the edge of a brimming well

They lose their sparkle
fall down like stones

# No

She says, “no, uncle”
the first time at the age six
when he pushes his tongue into her mouth
she trembles with unfamiliar fear

She says, “no, sir”
to her thesis professor
when he demands half an hour with drinks
Her refusal angers him. “I know your kind, you b…”
She gets up, throws her papers at his face
Humiliated, she walks out with fractured grace

She says, “no dear”
to her life partner, “not well, not today”
He understands perfectly well
He doesn’t argue but slaps her face hard
Her words suffocate at the hands of her lord

# Before It Breaks

Nervous pear tree watches
the penumbra sky
Sparrows wail
in shrill pitches

Furious winds suck
at the heavy bones
Rippled with pain
it bends like a samurai

# A Broken Kite

He follows me raising his index finger
a long spike dangling in front of my eyes
"Obey your master otherwise...remember"
An autumn leaf trembles

An ice cube pricks my black left eye
Ink bleeds down onto my cheek
A deep cut of upper swollen lip
hangs like a broken kite

His thorny hand-touch sends shivers
as he drags me to the bed
I choke under his heavy weight
my voice paralyzed

I sit on my haunches
in a bathtub   Hot water
stings like sharp needles   I burst
into uncontrollable sobs

My baby's soft bed
smells of my milk
I fold her into my arms
squeeze tight to my aching chest

I am a puppet
warped by tight string
My husband is the puppeteer
a cactus wrapped in silk.

London, England

# Beyond Closed Doors

Breath rattles like pinecones in my throat
I stumble into the shadows of fear
brush against a shroud of doubt

My eyes fix on rain-blotched windows
and the road where ghosts of vehicles
slice through the fog

In the distance an ambulance calls to me
Shuuub…Shuuub…Shuuub
Its echo dies in the stale air of the room

I wait for the sound of his footsteps
beyond the closed doors
for the rasp of his key in the locks

# दुःख

जाने क्या धोंद्ती रहेती हैः ये आंखे मुझ में
राख के ढेर में शोला है न चिंगारी

राख बर्बाद मोह्हबत की छपा राखी थी
बार बार छुआं तो बखिेर जायगी.

# Pain

What are your eyes searching for in me now?
All I have is a pile of ash from our volcanic past
that has neither fire nor spark
If you stir it again and again, it will scatter

Delhi, India

# Sweet Feeling of Freedom

I am in a caged room with iron bars
My bruised legs and stomach are painful
Why had the children kicked me so hard?

A girl in a white coat calls my name
Sasu someone wants to play with you
I listen but ignore her until she calls again

I turn my eyes at an angle, frowning
I see wide open arms and broad smile
I feel a little motion in my tail

I turn and walk slowly to the tall lady
My face is in her warm palms
She scratches my ears, looks into my eyes

I go with her to a house and take a bath
She soaps and rubs my black hair gently
I joyfully shake my coat and water drops flutter

Inside the house, I sniff all the corners
Drag my arse across the thick carpet
I scratch my back with the tree in the yard

I sunbathe with closed eyes on a porch
Get up and roll in the yard grass
I bend, I twist, I wiggle this or that way

I curl on the sofa in fluffy cushions
At night I sleep in my cushiony bed
In the morning she scratches my ears

She combs my fur, talks on the phone
says my name again and again
Soon I'm lolling on my back, legs in the air

# 3

# Prom

Trees rustle in a gust of wild hope
Their faded leaves crackle and swirl
giddy teenagers at the prom

Wild chimes shudder
Storm clouds turn violent

Strobe light blazes in the sky
as lightning spits
strikes my Bradford pear tree
turns it into an ashen coil

Other trees tremble like wildflowers
afraid they too will be asked to dance

# Chasm

Some relationships
don't break
even after parting hands
Feet keep chasing
rivers of time

Rivers shrink
between two banks
Massive monsoons
bend the shores
to their will

Shadows of heart
plough plants of sadness
Long sighs
buried under ribs
reverberating

I have placed on my tongue
a capsule of
your burning pain
It neither melts nor slides
scorches the back of the throat

(Note: A poem by the famous Indian poet, Gulzar, motivated me.)

# Restless Descents

An autumn sun
sinks behind skyscrapers
Heavy wings flap
to dusky refuges
Horn sickle moon
crescents on the scene

Restlessness descends
It's too long too long
since I had the luxury
of grieving

Come to me
Make me weep again
Let the anguish
console my heart

# Crab Constellation

Nothing much has changed
Her mumblings a dry well

Fickle as streetlights
ever-restless older son
waits impatiently to climb
the wall of affluence›

Younger son suffers
from a blood disorder
his malady crawling fast
through his shrinking frame

Growing girl's laughter
gurgles like a river
Her grief is a wild sea fever
Dark circles expand under her eyes

Father's ashes in the river
form a crab constellation
suffering and helpless poverty
Mother still cries in both her hands

Shantytowns, Addis Ababa, Ethiopia

# Season of Thorns

In the memory of desert
only cactus blooms

Anger waits inside
a secret fire

The deep breath inhales
inky shadows

Wave on wave
grief arrives and retreats

Every hurting word is a knife
goes deep and deep

Sorrow wears no mask
the eyes reflect gashes

Splintered dreams drink flame
slowly till ashen

How well then, the fire knows
the art of burning

# Melancholy

These barren branches
How the last leaf dangles on a ginkgo tree

How blue jay flaps its tense wings
on an unstrapped branch

The wet winding wind
sucks at the bones of the tree

then one branch cracks
falls to the ground

# Frame of Mind

Last night
the moon was blue
a silver star fell under my toe

Today beneath
the fallen sunrays
thorns tickle my ribs

Why do red roses bruise my eyes?
Why is wind knotted in my lungs?

# Microburst

Dogwood trees bend at the waist
Leaves break from the branches
chased like children by ghosts
Their bodies tremble in the alleys

The sky ruptures
A murderous rain rushes through the courtyards
drowning colorful hydrangeas

swamps city roads
carrying plastic bottles clothes
broken branches and shoes of children
in a whirling torrent

In the tomb of the city
the thunder echoes on rooftops
Lightning smears the faces of buildings
Parked cars bob and bob

Outside, fire trucks' shrill voices
reverberate like my own heart

# At Last

Leaves glisten
whisper into each others' ears
Meadowlarks orchestrate
a chorus of sparrows

Sprinkles stroke
the tormented grass
Rain falls from the eaves
dents the earth

Frogs take over the yard
with their rough croaks
Wilting roses gather drops
Their stems sway like ballerinas

Swollen clouds eclipse the sun
conspire with the wind
send chords of joy
rippling across the lake

Distressed trees
awake from their gloomy dream
as dry spell dragons
lose their footing

# Vertigo

Barrels of light
  collide
  sending splinters
  into my honeycomb eyes
  which pulse
  against the skin
  of my trembling palms

Panicked I fall on pillows
  drowning
  in swirling currents
  a gillless fish
  in turbulent water
  as ocean waves roll
  and break against my ears

Like a dropped coin I spin
  gelled eyes unfocused
  in a labyrinth of confusion
  every breath echoes
  in my lungs
  like bamboo chimes clattering
  in a sudden storm

# Purple Asters

A restless sun
paints patches of clouds
with a gold brush
The moon gathers strength
waking from its lingering sleep
in a tawny night

The wind curls— moans
over swarms of autumn leaves
fresh from the pear trees
Swirling cloaks of mist
turn bare branches
into swaying ghosts

In the lifting fog
moonbeams dance
across the brown grass
come to rest
on the last autumn flowers
those fallen stars

# Above McKinney Falls, Austin, TX

We are in a thicket
on a rock-studded trail
surrounded by old baldies
wide canopy's sparse
shadow across our paths

We slip down to a winding stream
that looks like a frail woman
shrunken by the weight of volcanic rocks
I pick up one to determine
whether its inner heart is still warm

The lacy cypress leaves
are swollen by the brume
that rises from the earth
licking and swallowing the greenery
in its dark maw

A slight shuffling of feathers in the brush
is the only sound in the arroyo
We return as quiet as the shawl
of incipient fog, conversing
only with our entwined hands

# The Smile

The smile brightens my face
it cures all aches
when lost
it becomes a melody I cannot sing

It cures my aches
and burns like a magic lamp
in a child's fairyland

When lost
it cuts deep gashes into my heart
tarnishes my dreams

It becomes a melody I cannot sing
the helpless twitch of a wounded bird
that can neither fly nor die

# I Own Her

I am Peeku. I lift my beak up, move my jaw to mimic. After much rehearsal, I have developed a sharp receptor to sing her words.

I get up in the morning and tweet for iPad. Bollywood peppy songs fill me with vibrato energy. When she takes iPad away, my mood turns sour. In a shrill voice I quaver music, music, music.

When my cage door opens, I come out sit on yellow ladder to thrum with red beads. With stretched wings, air beneath, I fly a hummingbird speed from one end of the house to the other. After five or six rounds, I settle on the entrance glass door perch. I look out at the chattering sparrows. That fluffy squirrel from cherry tree branches ogles me, moving her round eyes so fast. My loud warbling and feverish excitement fill the house. I love line dancing on a window bar just like a girl walking on a tight rope in a circus.

I sit on mummy's shoulder and peck on her left cheek, narrating outside scenes in my gibberish.

I slide gently on the front side of her green shirt pecking faster all the while looking at her and then fly to my cage. Glide swiftly from open cage roof to the swing, slip on the yellow high bar. Coquettishly, I peek into the mirror tilting my head, asking who is the most beautiful. Like any teenager, I too am very vain.

I go to my dinner bowl for supper. I push away apple slice with my beak. I love eating only millet seeds. The other day when my Dr. Lisa learnt about my food habits, she held me in her fist and looking into my eyes commented, “Peeku, you have an attitude.” I opened my beak wide and gripped her index finger.

My friend Abby is white. No, no not albino. She has grey blue crests on her neck and wings. We kiss beak to beak and our churlish talks are unending. I go out of my cage and try hard to free her from hers. I am younger but much smarter. After all I am a Blue Blood: hand-raised Australian spangled budgie with sunny yellow head, blue chest, long tapered aqua tail and yellowish white scalloped markings on the wings like a swan. Oh! My beak is white and not red like any vagabond cockerel.

# My Best Friends During the Pandemic

Invited by the breeze
gently knocking at my front door
Laced with mask and gloves, I go out
Sun, the healer warms my face

Oh, the purple lilies' satiny dance
Swollen buds of orange daylilies are half opened
Their long blades seesaw showing off
I gently hold one and twist its ears teasing

Flat tops of crepe myrtles
show off their new purple and green
Peppery sparrows sit in a group
singing sacred hymns inviting me
I inhale fresh air in my lungs and join them

Ah, roses cradle in the lap of thorns
kiss young freshly opened buds
Pear tree branches are filling with leaves
Grass beneath is ruffled by the breeze
Their slender blades sway shaking dew drops

I return home filled with joy and comfort
Toss my mask and wash  lather  rub  rinse my
  hands
I close my eyes in gratitude and say a prayer
for my near and dear ones for their safety
My prayers tremble in the air
as Peeku sings a welcoming song

# Garden Within a Garden, Zilker Park

Weeping willows bow
with the humble grace of *geisha*
while a cacophony of blue jays
and the throaty bark of grackles
echo against slumbering magnolia leaves

Ah! There a dragonfly sips
nectar of the China Rose.
And there! red and orange carp
glide from light to shade
under moon bridge

Transfixed by such beauty
a squirrel and I
tiptoe
through the garden
beneath a parchment sky

# Untitled Poem

Ideas float
like snowflakes
settle one by one
on the surface of the mind
string letters into garlands
of words

Poets squeeze these words
into stanzas
release them
like autumn leaves

At times ideas appear
slowly
like moss growing
on stones
like poets searching for titles

[this page intentionally blank]

# Epilogue

# Ode to My Teacher

*For Scott Wiggerman*

I marvel at the way your
mind pulls from me lines that rhyme
I thought that I was blind
until words began to chime
when you wanted me to shine

You told me about poetic quirks
how to study rhymes and beats
so I dug into the many works
of Oliver, Dickinson, and Keats
tried to decorate my blank sheets

You taught me craft as an artist
how to dress emotions and feelings
in the garb of odes and sonnets
with spontaneous flow with a meaning
where vowels and meters are dreaming

You said poetry was music from a muse
whether it lives with or without rhyme
Listen to how the waves and echoes use
the sound of the wind to make more valid
poems that might otherwise be pallid

Your imagination is a delight to behold
your poetic quality is mysterious gold
Your meter gleams and your rhyme shines
Your verses wink and the moon smiles
at your excellent writing style

# Notes

Several poems in this collection are trimerics, a form created by Charles A Stone, including "Aladdin's Lamp, "Undertow," and "Soaring."

<u>Spellbound</u>

This poem was inspired by the landscape of the Sintra Valley in Lisbon, Portugal

<u>Mango Delight</u>

Alfanso, langar, banarasi, dusehri,and chausa are names of famous Indian mangos.

<u>Magic Shoes</u>

The Hindi word for "firefly" is *jugnu*.

<u>Grandmother's Song</u>

The Hindi word for "turmeric" is *haldi*.

<u>I Own Her</u>

"Budgie" is short for *budgerigar*, a type of parakeet.

# Acknowledgments

I want to extend my thanks to the members of the Austin Poetry Study Group: Geoffrey Hall, Marcelle Kasprowicz, Christine Gilbert, Susan Corbin, Sarah Webb, Amy Greenspan, Tom Woodruff, John Mitchell, Mark Smolen, Holly Noelke, Nora Greenstein, Biondi, Tina Posner, Dora Robinson, Allyson Whipple, Loren Stell Kathleen Hall, and Christa Pandey whose invaluable feedback helped me with these poems.

I am especially grateful to my professional editor, Cindy Huyser, without whose tireless work this book would not have been possible.

Finally, I am very thankful to Phyllis Kimmel, who sat with me and proofread the final draft of the manuscript in Washington, DC.

Much appreciation also to the editors of the following publications in which versions of these poems have been published, sometimes in earlier versions or with a different title:

*Austin Chronicle*: “Pain”

*Big River Poetry Review*: “Forced Marriage”

*Blue Hole* (anthology of the Georgetown Poetry Festival): “Purple Asters”

*Enigmatist*: "The Doe's Message," "At Last the Dry Spell Breaks …"

*San Antonio Highway*: "Hill Country Drought"

*Still We Sing*: Voices on Violence Against Women (Dhauli Books, 2021): "No"

*Texas Poetry Calendar*: "Bathing Spree," "Garden Within a Garden, Zilker Park," "Greetings from Wimberley," "Hill Country Sonata," "My Friday Night Lights," "Royal Iris"

*Verbal Art*: "The Spa Ritual"

*Words & Worlds / Wörte & Welten*: "Leaf Peeping in Stowe, Vermont"

Earlier versions of several poems have also appeared in my chapbook, *Sacred River* (Sociosights Press, 2016).

The cover design is the author's own flower decoration with plum and cherry blossoms.

# About Atmosphere Press

Founded in 2015, Atmosphere Press was built on the principles of Honesty, Transparency, Professionalism, Kindness, and Making Your Book Awesome. As an ethical and author-friendly hybrid press, we stay true to that founding mission today.

If you're a reader, enter our giveaway for a free book here:

SCAN TO ENTER
BOOK GIVEAWAY

If you're a writer, submit your manuscript for consideration here:

SCAN TO SUBMIT
MANUSCRIPT

And always feel free to visit Atmosphere Press and our authors online at atmospherepress.com. See you there soon!

# About the Author

**Shubh** was born in W. Punjab and was raised and educated in Delhi, India. When she was seven years old, her father gifted her with a book of *Gitanjali*, a collection of poems by Rabindranath Tagore. These poems spoke deeply to her, inspiring her to start writing poetry herself. She earned a master's degree in social work from Delhi School of Social Work, Delhi University. Soon after, she entered into an arranged marriage. Because of her husband's job, she traveled all over the world and lived in many countries.

Finally, she settled in the United States and lived in Austin, Texas, for thirty years, where she pursued her passion for poetry. She joined a poetry critique class in Austin to develop her hobby. She was a member of the Writers League of

Texas, the Austin Poetry Society and the Poetry Society of Texas. Her poetry has appeared in *Borderlands*, *Texas Poetry Review*, *Di-Verse-City*, *Austin International Poetry Festival*, *Ardent*, *Poetry in the Arts*, *Texas Poetry Calendar*, *Galaxy of Verse*, *Enigmatist*, *Austin Chronicle*, *San Antonio Highway*, and *Big River Poetry Review* of Baton Rouge, Louisiana.

Printed in the USA
CPSIA information can be obtained
at www.ICGtesting.com
LVHW042045150124
769053LV00039B/968

9 798891 321120